NEW VANGUARD 259

US FLUSH-DECK DESTROYERS 1916–45

Caldwell, Wickes, and Clemson classes

MARK LARDAS

ILLUSTRATED BY JOHNNY SHUMATE &
JULIAN BAKER

OSPREY PUBLISHING

Bloomsbury Publishing Plc

PO Box 883, Oxford, OX1 9PL, UK

1385 Broadway, 5th Floor, New York, NY 10018, USA

E-mail: info@ospreypublishing.com

www.ospreypublishing.com

OSPREY is a trademark of Osprey Publishing Ltd

First published in Great Britain in 2018

© Osprey Publishing Ltd, 2018

A catalog record for this book is available from the British Library.

ISBN: PB 9781472819970; eBook 9781472819994;
ePDF 9781472819987; XML 9781472827517

18 19 20 21 22   10 9 8 7 6 5 4 3 2 1

Index by Alan Rutter
Typeset by PDQ Digital Media Solutions, Bungay, UK
Printed in China through World Print Ltd.

Osprey Publishing supports the Woodland Trust, the UK's leading woodland conservation charity. Between 2014 and 2018 our donations are being spent on their Centenary Woods project in the UK.

To find out more about our authors and books visit **www.ospreypublishing.com**. Here you will find extracts, author interviews, details of forthcoming events and the option to sign up for our newsletter.

AUTHOR'S DEDICATION

To my good friend and fellow modeler Mitch Michelson, in memory of his late wife Heather.

AUTHOR'S NOTE

The following abbreviations indicate the sources of the illustrations used in this volume:

IWM – Imperial War Museum, UK

NARA – National Archives

LOC – Library of Congress, Washington, D.C.

USN – United States Navy

USNHHC – United States Navy History and Heritage Command, Washington D.C.

AC – Author's Collection

Other sources are listed in full.

GLOSSARY

Cruiser stern – A hull design where the two sides of the ship meet at a point at the stern, creating a curved line at the stern.

Cruising aped – The speed at which a ship is designed to move with economical fuel consumption, typically between 15 and 22 knots for a warship.

Cutaway stern – A hull design where a transom meets the sides of the ship at the stern, resulting in a wider stern width.

Deckhouse – A structure that sits on the main weather deck.

Fantail – The aft portion of the ship, typically between the aft deckhouse and the stern.

Flank speed – The maximum combat speed of a warship.

Forecastle – The front one-quarter to one-fifth of a ship. The forecastle deck is the weather deck forward. On many ships the forecastle deck is higher than the main weather deck for better seakeeping.

Hedgehog – An antisubmarine mortar introduced in 1943. It has an array (typically four rows of six) of contact-fused bombs fired over the bow of a ship.

Hogging – The condition when there is greater buoyancy amidships than at the ends. The ends curve down like a banana, straining the hull.

K-gun – A depth-charge thrower that launches a depth charge off one side of a ship. They are typically mounted in pairs, one on each side of the ship.

Low-angle guns – Guns incapable of elevating higher than 30-45 degrees, making them incapable of effectively engaging aircraft.

Oerlikon – A 20mm antiaircraft gun licensed from a design developed by the Swiss armaments company Schweizerische Werkzeugmaschinenfabrik Oerlikon and used extensively during World War II.

Paravane – A form of towed underwater glider used to destroy naval mines.

RAMP – An acronym for Recovered Allied Military Property, used to describe USS *Stewart* when recovered from Japan after the war. The name *Stewart* could not be used because it had been assigned to a new US Navy warship, the destroyer escort *Stewart*.

Sagging – The condition when there is greater buoyancy at the ends of a ship than there is amidships. The middle curves down, "sagging", straining the hull.

Y-gun – A depth-charge launcher that can launch a depth charge off both sides of a ship. It was mounted centerline, with two angled arms to hold depth charges. The arms point to the sides, and form a "Y" shape.

CONTENTS

US FLUSH-DECK DESTROYERS 1916–45
Caldwell, Wickes, and Clemson classes

INTRODUCTION

On October 31, 1941, the United States Navy destroyer *Reuben James* was escorting an eastbound North Atlantic convoy. Dawn was breaking at the beginning of the *Reuben James*'s eighth day with convoy HX-156. Both left Argentia, Newfoundland, on October 22. The nearest land, Ireland, was 800 miles to the east.

USS *Reuben James* was part of the US Navy's Neutrality Patrol. Established to enforce American neutrality after World War II started, by mid-1941 its mission had changed to escorting British convoys as far as the Mid-Ocean Meeting Point, 300 miles east of *Reuben James*.

Reuben James was part of a five-destroyer US Navy support force. Launched in 1919, *Reuben James* was one of 273 Caldwell-, Wickes-, and Clemson-class destroyers mass-produced during and after World War I. Because all but three were constructed with four smokestacks, they were often called "four-pipers." By 1941, 177 remained, including three converted to banana boats, and 50 "lent" to Great Britain. Some had lost one or two of their distinctive "four pipes" following conversion to other purposes.

Distinctively American in appearance, these flush-deck destroyers were the best in the world when designed in 1916, but had been designed before

The *Reuben James* as it appeared during the early 1930s, when the flush-deck destroyer was still the most modern destroyer in the fleet. (USNHHC)

HMS *Daring*, built in 1893 and commissioned in 1895, was the first ship built as a torpedo boat destroyer. The name for this class would soon be shortened to "destroyer." *Daring* served in the Royal Navy for 17 years, being decommissioned and scrapped in 1912. (© IWM Q 21143)

World War I changed destroyers to antiaircraft and antisubmarine platforms. They were outdated before the final flush-deck destroyer was commissioned and obsolescent by 1939. When a new global conflict began, however, they were pressed into service filling gaps. There were never enough destroyers. *Reuben James* was one of two flush-deck destroyers in its support group.

HX-156 had been stalked by U-552 that night. Its lookouts had spotted the distinctive four-pipe silhouette, and its captain was under orders to avoid attacking American warships. Fifty flush-deckers were in British service, however, and U-552's skipper could not positively identify the destroyer as American. At 05:32 he fired two torpedoes at *Reuben James*.

One struck: *Reuben James* blew apart. The bow sank immediately. The after section floated for five minutes before sinking. After it sank, two armed depth charges on it exploded, killing sailors struggling in the water. By the time help arrived, only 46 survivors remained. The United States Navy had suffered its first combat loss of World War II – 38 days before the United States formally entered the war.

On that day, December 7, 1941, another flush-deck destroyer, USS *Ward*, fired the first shot at Pearl Harbor. Over the next four years, these old destroyers would serve throughout the globe, in a wide variety of roles. This is their story.

DESIGN AND DEVELOPMENT

The destroyer emerged as a warship type in the 1890s. The term "destroyer" was a contraction, short for "torpedo boat destroyer." The destroyer started as an antidote for another new warship type: the torpedo boat. Torpedo boats were warships designed to carry and launch the self-propelled torpedo, invented in 1866 by Robert Whitehead.

A single torpedo was capable of sinking the largest 19th-century warship and could be delivered by small, fast, easily built and cheap vessels. Since most navies depended on their battle line – composed of large, expensive and hard-to-replace battleships – ways had to be found to protect battleships from torpedo boats.

JAPANESE DESTROYER "SHIRAKUMO."

The Russo-Japanese War of 1904–05 underscored the importance of the destroyer. Surface torpedo attacks by Japanese destroyers crippled the Russian fleet at Port Arthur. The Japanese destroyer *Shirakumo* was part of the Imperial Japanese Navy in that war. (AC)

The solution was the destroyer. Larger than a torpedo boat, destroyers were armed with a battery of quick-firing guns capable of crippling a torpedo boat. They were equipped with large, powerful engines, giving the speed to catch the swift torpedo boat.

While destroyers proved excellent platforms for killing torpedo boats, they were also excellent platforms for carrying torpedoes. Because they were larger than torpedo boats, they had better sea-keeping capability, better range, and greater survivability. Soon the destroyer eclipsed the torpedo boat in most navies, in the United States Navy more than many others.

Destroyer Development to 1916

The first destroyers were built between 1892 and 1894 for the Royal Navy. These vessels were tiny by World War I standards, since all were under 300 tons. These were the first ships specifically built to counter the torpedo-boat threat and capable of keeping up with the battle fleet. The class was quickly copied by other navies. The Imperial Russian Navy commissioned its first destroyer in 1895. Germany, France, Italy, and Japan launched their first classes of destroyers in 1899. Although Germany called theirs *Hochsee-Torpedoboot* (high-seas torpedo boat) rather than torpedo-boat destroyers, they were functionally identical in size and armament to other first-generation destroyers.

All first-generation destroyers, regardless of nationality, were propelled by reciprocating steam engines powered by coal-fired boilers. Most had two propellers, a maximum speed ranging from 25 to 31 knots, and displaced between 350 and 600 tons. They typically carried two torpedo tubes, one or two guns between 65mm and 88mm in size, and two to four light guns between 20mm and 50mm.

The United States Navy was relatively late on the scene when it came to destroyers. The threat posed to American battleships by Spanish torpedo boats during the 1898 Spanish–American War underscored the need for torpedo-boat destroyers, but the first United States destroyer, Bainbridge-class USS *Decatur*, was not commissioned until 1902.

It was larger than many first-generation destroyers, displacing 420 tons, and carrying two 18in. torpedoes, two 3in. guns, and six 6-pounder (57mm) guns. Its maximum speed was 31 knots. The large gun armament allowed it to quickly disable torpedo boats, and its engines were one-third more powerful than contemporary destroyers of other nations. This would be a trend US destroyers would follow for many years.

Two new technologies were rapidly adopted in destroyer construction: steam-turbine propulsion and oil fuel. The steam turbine introduced in 1897 produced much more power per unit weight than the triple-expansion reciprocating steam engine. The turbine machinery was lighter than the reciprocating-engines cylinders, and the turbine offered higher mechanical efficiency than a reciprocating engine.

Oil fuel had three advantages. It had a higher specific energy than coal so you could get more heat out of each pound of fuel. As a liquid it could be pumped into the firebox. Human stokers did not need to feed fuel into the boiler. Additionally, it produced no ash. Coal ash needed to be removed from the firebox, reducing the efficiency of coal-fired boilers. By 1905, steam turbines and oil fuel were becoming standard in new destroyer design.

The second generation of destroyers, which emerged between 1904 and 1912, reflected the transition between coal-fired reciprocating engines and oil-fired boilers with turbines. With most nations, including the United States, the first class of destroyers built with turbine engines were coal-fired. Once the turbine proved its utility, oil fuel was adopted in a subsequent class. The Royal Navy completed the transition to oil-fired turbine-engine destroyers with the Tribal class built between 1907 and 1909.

The United States started this transition with the Smith-class destroyers built between 1908 and 1910, which had turbines but burned coal, while the subsequent Paulding-class built between 1910 and 1912 added oil fuel. France, Russia, and Italy followed a similar pattern, abandoning coal, while Germany and Japan lagged behind. The first Japanese destroyer exclusively

The first destroyers built for the US Navy were the Bainbridge-class built between 1899 and 1902. They displaced only 420 tons, and had a top speed of 29 knots. *Chauncey* (shown below) was the third Bainbridge-class destroyer built. It sank in 1917 after colliding with a merchantman off Gibraltar. (USNHHC)

fueled with oil appeared in 1913, while Germany's first entirely oil-fired destroyer was launched in 1914.

The second generation was also larger than the first. They ranged from 500 to 750 tons, and carried four to eight torpedo tubes, doubling to quadrupling the striking power of earlier destroyers. The gun battery increased in size and number, with ships carrying up to four main guns, with bore sizes increasing to 4in. Speeds increased, too. By 1912, a slow destroyer could make 28 knots, and some classes could reach 36 knots.

A third generation emerged between 1912 and 1916. These added geared turbines. A propeller is most efficient at relatively low revolutions, while turbine efficiency increases with speed. At first, direct-drive turbines were used, with the propellers running at the speed of the engine. This compromised performance as the speed was too fast for efficient propellers, but too slow to get the best performance out of a turbine. A gear-box was added to slow the propeller rotation.

Gears required space and weight, and increased costs significantly, but the performance gained exceeded the penalties incurred. Destroyer size again jumped, with ships ranging from 750 to 1,100 tons. These were as fast as the smaller ships, were better sea boats, and could carry more torpedo tubes. The final class of US "1,000-tonner" destroyers, the Sampson-class of 1915, carried 12 torpedo tubes in triple mountings and could reach 29.5 knots.

As 1916 opened, the United States Navy decided it needed to go bigger still, seeking to produce the ultimate destroyer, one superior to that of every other navy: the Caldwell class.

Caldwell Class

When the United States Navy General Board, the organization responsible for ship design, drafted requirements for a destroyer in 1915, it needed to satisfy a number of mutually exclusive needs.

The Navy's senior admirals wanted a destroyer with a good range, high speed, improved seakeeping ability, and a balance between the offensive possibilities of torpedoes and the defensive capabilities provided by guns.

The Sampson-class, known as "1,000-tonners" for their designed displacement, was the final class of US destroyers built prior to the introduction of the flush-deck destroyers. This is the Sampson-class USS *Davis*, on escort duty in World War I. (USNHHC)

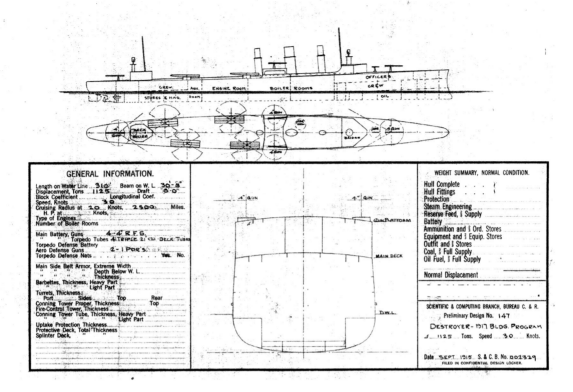

They also wanted a destroyer capable of scouting, a role normally filled by light cruisers. The United States Navy lacked light scout cruisers. This required a destroyer larger than the 1,000-tonners then currently being built by the Navy.

The Navy's destroyer officers wanted a small vessel optimized for torpedo attacks. They advocated a return to the size of the 750-ton second-generation "Flivvers" (named after that period's nickname for a small automobile in the US) built between 1908 and 1912, upgraded with the latest technology. A smaller vessel made with a reduced profile would be harder to hit. Centerline torpedo tubes, using the triple-mounts developed earlier, gave a bigger maximum torpedo salvo than the old flivvers with their wing-mounted twin-mounts.

Range was important for United States Navy operations. Most other navies faced littoral opponents. The Imperial German Navy planned to meet its foes in the North Sea or Baltic Sea. France optimized its navy to fight in the English Channel, the Bay of Biscay, and the Mediterranean Sea. Japan's attention was focused on the Sea of Japan and the China Sea. Russia had separate fleets for the Baltic, the Black Sea, and the Far East. While the Royal Navy spanned the entire globe, Britain concentrated its ships in the North Sea, the Mediterranean, and the Channel. Outside European waters, the Royal Navy was content to show the flag with one or two warships. Its major battles were expected to be fought in the North Sea, Mediterranean, or English Channel, with bases within a day or two's steaming.

The United States Navy enjoyed no such luxury. The US Navy wargamed scenarios against potential opponents, who included Germany, Japan, and Britain (the latter mostly because it was the world's largest navy, not in any

The Caldwell class had their origins in the "Destroyer-1917 Building Program" initiated by the US Navy in 1915. The initial design, shown here, used all the lessons of destroyer operations prior to 1914, but did not incorporate 1915 and 1916 wartime experiences. (USNHHC)

The Japanese counterpart to the flush-deck destroyer was the Momi class, built between 1918 and 1923, and smaller than the flush-deck destroyers. The Japanese subsequently built larger destroyers. By World War II, most surviving Momi-class ships had been downrated to patrol boats. (AC)

real expectation of war). All plans involved long voyages, whether to meet European opponents in the mid-Atlantic or in the Caribbean, or sending naval relief forces to Hawaii or the Philippines. Some envisioned operations at distances from the nearest port. Scenarios and exercises requiring ships with ranges of 2,000 nautical miles were typical.

Long range and operations in open ocean required larger vessels, both for seakeeping and to allow sufficient bunker space for fuel. Destroyer men, seeking a smaller vessel, believed their destroyers could be towed by other warships over open ocean when long voyages were required, preserving fuel for battle. The Navy Board was less confident of the practicality of that solution, however.

The resulting design released by the Navy Board in September 1915 for its FY1917 destroyer was large: 310ft on the waterline and displacing 1,125 tons. It had a top speed of 30 knots and a cruising radius of 2,500 miles steaming at 20 knots. It also carried a heavy battery: 12 torpedoes in four wing-mounted triple-tube mounts, and four 4in./50-caliber deck guns. Two guns were centerline-mounted on the forecastle and quarterdeck. Two waist guns were mounted on platforms above the deck, with the galley between them. For defense against aircraft, it would carry two high-angle one-pounders, considered more than adequate in 1915.

By contrast, destroyers being built by other nations in 1915 were considerably weaker. The British M-classes displaced 850-994 long tons and carried four 21in. torpedo tubes and three 4in. guns. The Japanese Momi-class, built in 1916, displaced 848 tons and mounted six 21in. torpedo tubes and three 4in. guns.

The FY1917 design had four boilers in two fire-rooms amidships. The draft design showed three funnels, with the uptakes of the middle boilers trunked together. The engine room was immediately behind the boiler rooms. Propulsion was a departure from the US standard. This destroyer had three screws. The center propeller was driven by a cruise engine, which provided power for its 20-knot cruise speed. The port and starboard engines were engaged when the 30-knot flank speed was required.

The most revolutionary and distinctive feature of the design was the lack of a forecastle deck. A high forecastle was necessary for seakeeping, but the requirement for high speed dictated a shallow draft. A towering forecastle and shallow hull aft of the forecastle was virtually a trademark characteristic of a destroyer.

This design was wider than previous US destroyers, which required a shallower draft. The new hull form was expected to reduce rolling and pitching. The conventional forecastle design caused the midship hull box to be too shallow, resulting in a weak hull. The forecastle deck continued the length of the ship, with the run of the deck at an angle to the waterline. The resulting flush-deck design was deeper at the bow than the stern.

This design also had a ram bow as an antisubmarine defense. (Depth charges had not yet been invented.) The chart house replaced the forward searchlight platform of the previous destroyer design, giving the bridge better access to it. The additional equipment on the deck reduced the size of the aft deckhouse, squeezing out the radio room from its traditional location. The radio room was moved to the forward deckhouse, a change that made the radio more accessible to bridge crew, and was retained in future designs.

USS *Caldwell* (Destroyer No. 69) was the lead ship in its class. It lacked the ram bow, triple propellers, and trunked middle funnel of the Destroyer-1917 design, but was similar otherwise. This shows *Caldwell* fitting out at Mare Island, one month prior to commissioning in December 1917. (USNHHC)

Six destroyers were authorized. Two were built at Navy yards (the class namesake USS *Caldwell* at Mare Island and USS *Craven* at Norfolk Navy Yard). Four were contracted to private builders. William Cramp at Philadelphia built two (USS *Connor* and *Stockton*), Seattle Dry Dock Company built USS *Gwin*, and Bath Iron Works, in Maine, built USS *Manley*.

These ships were viewed as prototypes, and no two were completely identical. All differed from the FY1917 design in some particulars. All eliminated the ram bow. *Gwin*, *Connor*, and *Stockton* followed the three-funnel and three-screw arrangement of the Navy Board design. *Caldwell*, *Craven*, and *Manley* reverted to the traditional two-propeller configuration, and simplified construction by exhausting each boiler with a separate smokestack, yielding the characteristic four-pipes later construction would use.

Wickes Class

In 1916, the United States declared war on Germany and entered World War I as an Allied Power. Before World War I, the United States Navy procured ships in small batches. The six destroyers authorized for the Caldwell class was typical. Suddenly the United States Navy needed lots of ships, including many destroyers.

The Wickes-class was the first mass-produced United States Navy destroyer. This shows four under construction at the New York Shipbuilding Corporation shipyard in Camden, NJ. Left to right: *Leary* (Destroyer No. 158), *Babbitt* (Destroyer No. 128), *Dickerson* (Destroyer No. 157), and *Jacob Jones* (Destroyer No. 130). All four were completed after World War I, but played significant roles during World War II. (USNHHC)

The Navy Board decided the solution lay in mass producing destroyers to a common design. The design used was based on the Caldwell class. In many ways, the Caldwell class represented the pinnacle of destroyer design in 1915. They would have been perfect destroyers for Jutland. They could scout out the area. They could dash in against the enemy battle line to fire salvoes of six torpedoes each – twice – and then protect their battle line from enemy torpedo attack with 4in. quick-firing guns.

Yet a design that was perfect in 1915 already held shortcomings by 1916. It had little antiaircraft strength and no antisubmarine capability. The main battery used low-angle guns, incapable of being used against aircraft, and the two planned 1.1in. machine guns were inadequate even in World War I. And by 1916 destroyers were emerging as the most important ship for fighting submarines. But the design was available, and ships were needed quickly. The result was the Wickes class, slightly modified versions of the Caldwell class.

Wickes retained the same general arrangements as the Caldwell-class destroyers. It was slightly longer – 314ft 4.5in. against the 308ft waterline length of the Caldwells – and shared the same general arrangement of guns and torpedoes. To simplify construction, it reverted to the twin-screw design, abandoning the center propeller. It also had a knife-edge cruiser stern rather than the cutaway stern of the Caldwells.

 USS *STOCKTON* (DD73) IN WORLD WAR I

USS *Stockton* was one of six Caldwell-class destroyers. Each Caldwell differed. *Stockton* may have been the most unusual flush-deck destroyer of them. It and its sister, *USS Conner* (DD-72), were built with three funnels; the exhaust for the center two boilers were trunked together in a single, fat, central funnel.

Additionally, they had three propellers; a center shaft was turned by a high-pressure geared turbine and two outer propellers ran off a direct-drive medium-pressure steam turbine. *Stockton* could run under the center propeller when cruising, to save fuel. *Stockton* was also experimentally armed with a twin 4in./50-cal. mount forward.

Stockton was in commission with the US Navy from 1918 to 1922. It served in World War I, being stationed out of Brest, France. It was turned over to the Royal Navy as part of the Destroyers-for-Bases swap in 1940. It served in the Royal Navy as HMS *Leeds* from October 1940 to April 1945.

This plate shows *Stockton* as it appeared in 1918, painted in a distinctive dazzle camouflage pattern of that period.

Displacement:	1,010 tons (normal), 1,125 tons (full load)
Dimensions:	315ft 6in. x 31ft 4in. x 8ft 1in.
Propulsion:	2 direct drive medium-pressure Parsons steam turbines, one geared high-pressure Parsons steam turbine (3 shafts), 4 × 300psi boilers, 18,500shp (designed)
Speed:	30 knots
Fuel:	Oil
Crew:	146 officers, petty officers, and sailors
Armament (1918):	5 4in./50-caliber guns (3x1 1x2), 12 × 21in. torpedo tubes (4 × 3), 2 depth-charge racks

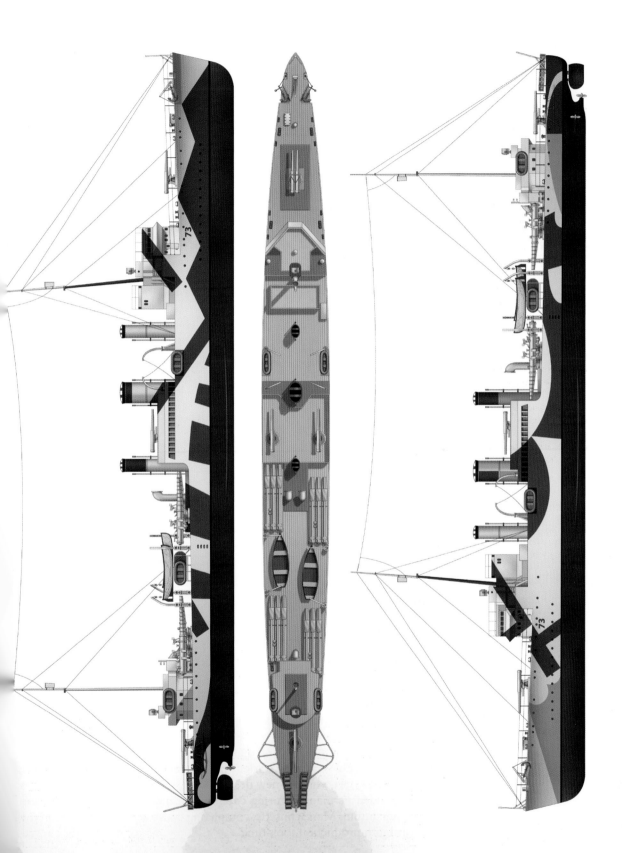

Construction of some Wickes-class ships occurred at a blistering pace. *Ward* (Destroyer No. 139) took only 17 days between keel-laying and launching. *Ward* is shown immediately before launch at Mare Island Navy Yard, on June 1, 1918. (USNHHC)

The main difference between the two classes was their speed. The earlier destroyers could only generate 20,000 shaft horsepower, giving them a top speed of 30 knots. The Wickes-class had larger boilers, with a higher maximum pressure, which increased the horsepower generated by the boiler by one-third. Improved reduction gearing increased the useful power sent to the propellers. The hull design was modified to reduce drag.

The result was a destroyer which could reach 35 knots and keep up with the planned 35-knot battle-cruisers and light cruisers authorized in the same appropriations bill. Unlike earlier naval appropriations, the 1916 appropriations ordered ships on a grand scale.

Fifty Wickes-class destroyers were authorized; 20 to be built in 1917, the rest to be completed later. The bill also allowed another 15 destroyers to be added at the request of the President. Before 1916 ended, that 15 and another 11 were requested. As the scope of the U-boat threat became more obvious and the need for destroyers grew, additional Wickes destroyers were ordered. In all, 111 were ordered and eventually built.

The biggest challenge faced was building this number of ships. At the time the appropriation bill passed, not one Caldwell-class vessel had been laid down, yet the Navy was ordering 50 more destroyers. The Navy distributed the work to eight shipyards. Bath Iron Works got contracts for eight, and Cramp received orders for 21. Newport News in Virginia got 11; New York Shipbuilding in Camden, NJ, got ten. Union Iron Works in San Francisco and Fore River Shipyard in Quincy, Massachusetts (both owned by Bethlehem Steel) bagged 52 ships, 26 at each. Finally, Navy yards built nine: eight at Mare River and one at Charleston.

Each shipyard received common plans from the Navy, but each contractor had individual variations, and each used different boilers and turbines. The 52 ships built at Bethlehem Steel-owned shipyards used Yarrow boilers and Curtis turbines. Bath favored boilers manufactured by Normand, Thornycroft, or White-Foster with Parsons turbines, a choice imitated by all other civilian yards and the two Navy yards. The limiting item slowing construction proved to be the reduction gearing. Newport News avoided this problem by omitting the gears and installing direct-drive turbines.

The gear bottleneck was only one production bottleneck, however. Some yards had merchant construction on their existing ways, while several other shipyards had other warships started. Even when this work was suspended, it took time to start work on new destroyers. Additionally, while Bethlehem Steel expanded its manufacturing capabilities, including adding a ten-slip yard at Squantum, Massachusetts, completing construction and bringing the new yard into production took time.

The first Wickes-class destroyer, USS *Little*, was not launched until November 11, 1917, and not commissioned until April 6, 1918. Only five were launched before 1918 began, and by Armistice Day, November 11, 1918, just 38 were in commission, of which nine had entered service before July 1, 1918. Construction of five began only after the war ended. Construction continued, however, and the last member of the class was not launched until September 1919. One ship, USS *Tillman*, was finally commissioned in April 1921.

The operational shortcomings of the Wickes class became apparent even before the first vessel was commissioned. One of the first changes was installation of stern depth-charge racks to provide antisubmarine capability. The narrow stern and the aft gun, also located on the fantail, constricted the space available for depth-charge racks, however.

Experience also revealed other problems with gun placement. The fantail aft gun proved too wet at high speed or with high waves. Over time, this gun would be relocated to the top of the aft deckhouse. The beam guns were unable to point closer than 30 degrees from the bow. This left only one 4in. gun capable of firing forward. The Navy experimented with adding a twin 4in. mount in the bow, but only mounted a few experimentally. The 1.1in. antiaircraft gun ran into production difficulties, and too few were available. A 3in./23-caliber antiaircraft gun was substituted.

The biggest shortcoming was range. A Wickes-class vessel was supposed to steam 3,600 nautical miles (nm) at 15 knots. Actual performance depended on the building yard, however. Bath boats could steam 3,990nm at 15 knots, but USS *Gregory*, built at Fore River, could only manage 2,300nm. Even as various shipyards were lurching their way to full production, the Navy realized it needed both more destroyers and better destroyers. The result was the Clemson class.

Clemson Class

The Clemson class started as an effort to create an improved destroyer but ended as a slightly modified Wickes class. In July 1917, the Navy put out a request for a destroyer armed like the Wickes class, but capable of using mines and depth charges, and able to steam 4,000nm at 15 knots. A top speed of 28 knots was requested. It was intended as an escort vessel, the World War I equivalent of what became the destroyer escort in World War II.

The Navy decided to address other issues as well. The new British V- and W-class destroyers were being built

A major construction issue with Bethlehem Steel shipyard-built ships – on both coasts – was the boilers installed. Built by Yarrow Boiler Works (shown), they proved short-lived. The Navy scrapped 60 active flush-deck destroyers with Yarrow boilers in 1930 because replacing their worn-out boilers was uneconomical. (USNHHC)

with four 4.7in. guns, all on the centerline, outgunning the US destroyers. Additionally, new German U-boats were rumored to be carrying 5in. deck guns. The US Navy decided to arm this new class of destroyers with a 5in. battery.

The problem was the United States Navy needed more destroyers yesterday. The Navy spent two months developing their new design, but builders approached about construction objected, emphasizing any major change would delay construction. The Navy Board, unenthusiastic about the new design's lower speed, quashed it, reprising the Wickes design.

There were very few differences between the two classes. In the Clemson class, the deck was strengthened to allow mounting 5in./51-caliber guns. Bunkers tanks for an additional 100 tons of oil were added, increasing range by 1,200nm at 15 knots. A larger rudder was added to improve steering. The main mast was shortened to increase the coverage zone of the

B HMS *CAMPBELTOWN*, MARCH 1942

One of the best-known flush-deck destroyers was HMS *Campbeltown*, a Wickes-class destroyer traded to Great Britain in 1940 and expended in the St Nazaire Raid on March 28, 1942.

The ship was used in Operation *Chariot*, a British attack on the Normandie Dock at St Nazaire. The lock was the only drydock outside of German home waters capable of holding the German battleship *Tirpitz*, so its destruction would force *Tirpitz* to return to Germany for repairs if damaged in an Atlantic sortie. The raid envisioned ramming an explosives-packed *Campbeltown* into the lock at the entrance to the drydock and exploding it.

This plate shows *Campbeltown*'s appearance following conversion to a demolition ship. Its bow was filled with 24 British Mark VII depth charges, 9,000lb of amatol, hidden in a steel and concrete case below the forward gun. Its original armament was removed – guns, torpedo tubes, and depth charges. These were replaced with a 12-pounder gun at the forward gun position and eight 20mm Oerlikons. The bridge was armored, and plating was added amidships on the decks to protect the commandos aboard.

In an effort to fool the Germans, the profile of *Campbeltown* was altered to resemble a German Raubvogel-class torpedo boat. This involved removing the two after funnels and raking the two forward funnels. As can be seen by comparing the altered *Campbeltown* to the profile of a Raubvogel-class torpedo boat above the *Campbeltown* in the plate, the deception would only have worked on a very dark night from a very long distance.

Given the appearance of *Campbeltown* when it entered Royal Navy service (drawn to scale, superimposed behind the *Raubvogel* profile), a more convincing deception could have been achieved by removing the second and third funnel and trimming the fourth funnel. Regardless, *Campbeltown* succeeded in destroying the Normandie Dock when it exploded after dawn on March 28.

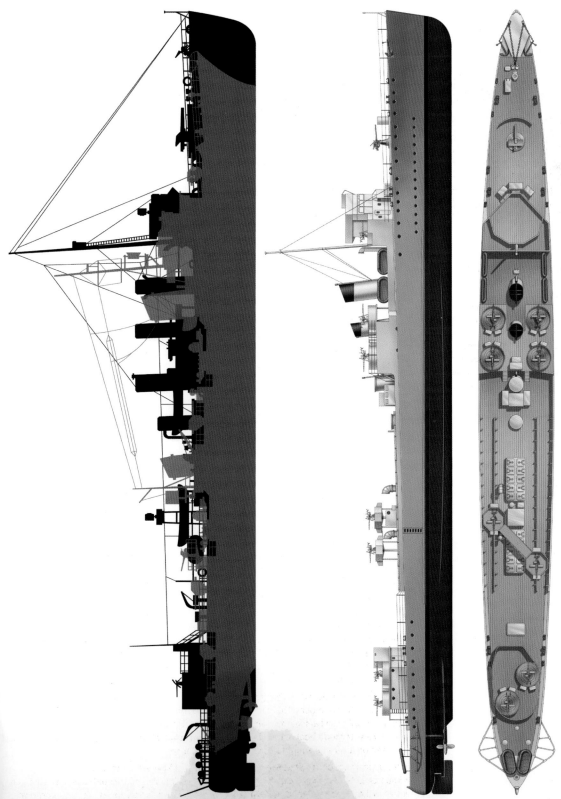

While the United States perfected the flush-deck design, Great Britain used its wartime experience in building its wartime V- and W-classes. The later classes, with 4.7in. guns and 40mm antiaircraft guns, were superior to the flush-deck destroyer in overall utility. (AC)

aft 3in./23-caliber antiaircraft gun. (This modification was also made to the Wickes-class ships after World War I ended.)

Antisubmarine armament was also beefed up. Y-gun depth-charge launchers were added, which could launch depth charges broadside. These were added to all flush-deck classes starting in July 1918.

The Clemson class reprised many of the flaws of the Wickes class, however. It still had a wide turning circle at flank speed, and the antiaircraft battery was inadequate.

The Navy ordered 161 of this new class of destroyer. Bethlehem Steel would build 85 at its shipyards in Quincy, Squantum, and San Francisco, Cramp 25, Newport News 14 (with geared turbines), New York Shipyard 20, Bath Iron Works three, and the United States Navy nine (six at Mare Island and three at Norfolk Naval Yard). Five were canceled before construction began.

Only 64 had been started when World War I ended on November 11, 1918, and none had yet been commissioned. (USS *Delphy* DD-261, the first to enter service, was commissioned on November 30, 1918.) The Navy had all but the canceled five completed. The final Clemson-class destroyer, DD-341, USS *Decatur*, was not completed until August 1922.

Building destroyers from a 1915 design well into the 1920s was a curious decision. The late-war British destroyers of the W-class and modified W-class were superior to the Clemson class in just about every category except the total number of torpedo tubes mounted. Japan, already emerging as the United States' main naval rival, spent the postwar years building new classes of destroyers, absorbing the lessons of World War I.

As the United States was finishing the last of the flush-deck destroyers, Japan was laying down the keels of the Kamikaze class, ships displacing 1,400 tons and mounting a broadside of four 120mm guns. By contrast, the United States now had a fleet of several hundred new but essentially outdated destroyers. The United States Navy would not build a new class of destroyer for another decade, when the Farragut class was laid down in 1932.

To speed up production, Bethlehem Steel built the Victory Destroyer Plant at Squantum, Massachusetts. Thirty-five Clemson-class destroyers were built there, including *Bailey* and *Morris*, shown in the wet slips. All were completed after World War I. (USNHHC)

OPERATIONAL HISTORY

The first flush-deck destroyer was commissioned in October 1917; the last flush-deck destroyer was laid up in 1950. In a brief 33-year history, they steamed on every ocean and accomplished great things.

World War I: 1916–19

The United States declared war on Germany on April 6, 1917. On that date, work had started on only four flush-deck destroyers: *Caldwell*, *Connor*, *Stockton*, and *Manley*. These four destroyers, all Caldwell-class, were all commissioned between October 1917 and January 1918. They would see extensive service during World War I. The other pair in the class, *Craven* and *Gwin*, were completed too late to see action in World War I.

The Wickes class fared little better. Three – *Wickes*, *Little*, and *Kimberly* – were laid down in June 1917. Four more were started in July, and construction started on a total of 40 before December 1917 ended. Work on five Wickes-class destroyers did not start until after November 11, 1918, and only 36 Wickes-class destroyers were in commission on Armistice Day. Of those, only half entered the combat zone. Of the seven destroyers built on the Pacific Coast in commission on November 11, 1918, only *Fairfax* and *Taylor* arrived in the Atlantic soon enough to take part in the war. Of those built on the Atlantic Coast, 11 of the 29 destroyers commissioned before November 11 took part in the war. The rest were completing shakedown cruises or awaiting assignment when the guns ceased firing.

Construction of the Clemson-class ships did not even begin until mid-April in 1918. Only one, USS *Delphy*, laid down on April 20, 1918, and launched on July 18, was in commission in 1918. It entered service on November 30, three weeks after the war's end. Work on most ships of the Clemson class did not begin until the war was over. Only 65 of the 156 ships built had been laid down by Armistice Day.

Yet while most of the load carried by United States Navy destroyers was carried by the pre-war Flivvers and 1,000-tonners, the flush-deck destroyers played a small but significant part in the war. They came into their own in

Twenty-two flush-deck destroyers saw combat during World War I. None received combat damage, although several were damaged in accidents and collisions. This is the USS *Stockton* after ramming the steamship *Slieve Bloom* off the South Sark Light. (USNHHC)

the months between the November 11 ceasefire date and the signing of the Treaty of Versailles on July 28, 1919, when the war officially ended. The most active flush-deck destroyers were the four completed Caldwell-class ships along with the first Wickes-class ships commissioned: *Little, Fairfax, Kimberly, Sigourney, Stevens, Gregory,* and *Rathburne.*

Eleven flush-deckers were stationed in Europe. Five – *Connor, Little, Fairfax, Sigourney,* and *Gregory* – operated out of Brest, France. They provided part of the escort protecting transports carrying United States troops to the Western Front. Five others – *Caldwell, Stockton, Manley, Kimberly,* and *Stephens* – worked out of Queenstown, Ireland, guarding supply convoys steaming to Britain.

USS *Dyer* was sent to Gibraltar in July, reinforcing five ancient Bainbridge-class destroyers stationed there escorting Mediterranean convoys. USS *Luce* joined *Dyer* in October, and *Gregory* transferred to Gibraltar on November 2, when German U-boat activity in the Mediterranean increased. Four other destroyers – *Taylor, Colhoun, Stringham,* and *Talbot* – escorted at least one convoy across the Atlantic, while *Wickes, Bell,* and *Rathburne* guarded ships traveling in the coastal waters of the United States and Canada.

The work done by these ships was routine, tedious, and occasionally dangerous. Most consisted of convoy protection. Because they were the largest and best-equipped US destroyers, a flush-deck destroyer assigned to a convoy usually served as the escort flagship. Occasionally they served other functions, escorting or transporting senior officials.

The flush-deck destroyers failed to sink any German U-boats during their escort services, but did see action. In March 1918, *Stockton,* in company with the 1,000-tonner *Ericsson,* attacked a U-boat while escorting the troopship *St Paul* from Queenstown to Liverpool. *Stockton* avoided a torpedo fired at it, dropping depth charges on its attacker. The U-boat got away safely,

One unusual service for flush-deck destroyers during World War I was transporting senior officials. USS *Dyer* carried then-Assistant Secretary of the Navy Franklin D. Roosevelt to Europe. The ship is shown as Roosevelt's flagship at the Azores. (USNHHC)

but so did the troopship. *Connor* rescued survivors from torpedoed freighters twice in July 1918. *Stringham* drove off a U-boat attacking the Brazilian steamship *Uberaba* in August 1918. On October 18, 1918, *Fairfax* rescued 86 survivors of the torpedoed American cargo ship *Lucia*.

The flush-deckers suffered injury while on escort duty, although not through enemy action. On March 19, 1918, *Stockton* collided with a merchantman near the South Sark Light. A more serious casualty also occurred in March. While escorting a convoy, *Manley* almost collided with a large transport while closing to deliver orders. A collision was averted, but the wake of the 6,000-ton steamer swept two armed depth charges off *Manley*'s stern racks. They exploded under its stern, crippling *Manley* and killing 34 members of its crew. *Manley* was towed to Queenstown and repaired, but was not back in service until December 1918. *Wickes*, too, was injured in a collision with a merchant ship while escorting a convoy off New York in October 1918.

The only damage suffered by a flush-deck destroyer as a result of enemy weapons from World War I happened two years after the war's end. USS *Kane*, cruising in the Baltic in October 1920, struck a drifting mine. As with *Manley*, the damage was repaired after a six-month stay in Swedish and British dockyards.

Escorting destroyers had no means of detecting submerged U-boats. In 1918, sonar was in its infancy, being tested experimentally by Britain and France. *Caldwell* and *Colhoun* both participated in testing sound equipment near the end of the war. While sonar had to wait until World War II for operational service, the flush-deck destroyers helped prove it.

The armistice did not end convoy duties. Mistrust of the Central Powers and the spate of revolutions in Eastern Europe kept US Navy destroyers escorting individual ships and convoys through the first half of 1919, especially in waters formerly controlled by the Central Powers. The flush-deck destroyers entering service replaced older, less capable US destroyers as they finally arrived.

Other postwar duties kept the flush-deck ships busy prior to the signature of the Versailles Treaty. No fewer than nine flush-deck destroyers participated in escorting the convoy carrying President Woodrow Wilson to France for the peace conference in May 1919. In May 1919, the United States Navy attempted the first transatlantic flight, using three Curtis flying boats to make the voyage. One, NC-4, completed the mission. Twenty-one flush-deck destroyers served as airplane guards on the third leg of the flight. Spaced 50nm apart, they formed a bridge of boats from Flores in the Azores to Mistaken Point, Newfoundland.

USS *Craven*, a Caldwell-class ship, was commissioned on October 18, 1918, too late to participate in combat. It is shown here in dazzle camouflage, dressed with flags celebrating Armistice Day. (USNHHC)

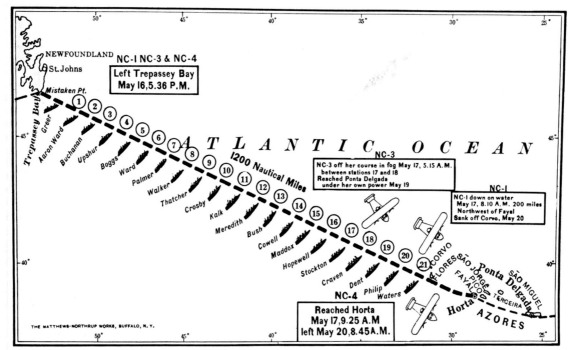

Third Leg, U. S. Navy Flying Boats NC-3, NC-1 and NC-4 from Trepassey Bay to Azores.
(Time given is New York Standard)

Twenty-one flush-deck destroyers served as airplane guards during the US Navy's first and successful attempt to fly aircraft across the Atlantic. The map shows the names of the destroyers and their positions. (USNHHC)

Between the Wars: 1919–39

The signing of the Versailles Treaty marked the beginning of the flush-deck destroyers' glory days. The design might have been a touch outdated, but they were the newest destroyers in existence. Great Britain was winding down destroyer construction. Japan used the years immediately after World War I to appraise destroyer design. The United States building program continued unabated between 1919 and 1921, when the last flush-decked destroyer was commissioned. There were so many new flush-deck destroyers available that by 1922, every destroyer from all earlier classes of United States Navy destroyer was laid up in reserve. With the exception of four thousand-tonners reactivated for service in the Coast Guard during prohibition and one thousand-tonner used as a training ship, none saw further service.

In fact, there were too many flush-deck destroyers for the Navy to use. Scores finished one commission following construction and went into the reserve fleet in 1922 to await further need. Most Wickes-class ships ended up in reserve, and many of the remaining ships were commissioned with half-crews or with one crew alternating between two destroyers. While many mothballed ships saw service in the 1930s or were reactivated for World War II, nearly three dozen were scrapped, seeing no further service.

The flush-deck destroyers in commission during the early 1920s saw the world. Flush-deck destroyers traveled everywhere, including waters the US Navy would not revisit until after the end of the Cold War. There were squadrons of flush-deck destroyers on both American coasts, stationed in the Caribbean, Hawaiian waters, and in the Far East, where the flush-deck destroyers made up the backbone of the Asiatic Fleet. Squadrons patrolled

the Black, Baltic, and Arctic Seas supporting the Allied intervention in the Russian Civil War between 1919 and 1922.

The flush-deck destroyers in the Black Sea also supported operations in the Aegean and Eastern Mediterranean. They provided humanitarian support during the war between Greece and Turkey in the years following World War I. This covered a variety of tasks: carrying medicine and relief supplies, evacuating civilians from besieged cities, transporting diplomats, and assisting distressed ships. In December 1922, the Clemson-class *Bainbridge* rescued 482 people from a burning French transport in the Sea of Marmara. Exploding ammunition made the rescue hazardous, and the operation earned *Bainbridge*'s captain, Lt Commander Walter A. Edwards, a Medal of Honor.

The speed and relatively low cost of operation of flush-deck destroyers made them a natural fit for relief operations throughout the 1920s and 1930s. In 1920, USS *Harding* took bubonic plague serum from New Orleans to Tampico and Vera Cruz, Mexico, ending a plague outbreak. Following the 1923 Great Kanto Earthquake, USS *Noa* and *John D. Edwards* rushed medicine and food to Yokohama. Flush-deck destroyers were also sent to rescue Western missionaries in China from disorders resulting from the various revolutionary movements during the 1920s and 1930s. When the Army made its round-the-world flight in 1924, numerous flush-deck destroyers served as airplane guards along the route.

Despite the hazards offered by World War I and the fratricidal combat of its aftermath, the first flush-deck destroyer lost was lost in a peacetime accident. On February 26, 1921, Wickes-class USS *Woolsey* was rammed and sunk by the SS *Steel Inventor* off the Pacific coast of Panama. Over the next three years, losses came thick and fast. On December 1, 1921, while operating with 50 percent of her crew, USS *De Long* ran aground on Halfmoon Bay near San Francisco. It was refloated, towed to Mare Island and scrapped. USS *Graham* was the next loss, rammed by SS *Panama* off New Jersey.

USS *John D. Edwards* was one of 156 Clemson-class destroyers built for the United States Navy. It was built by William Cramp & Sons at Philadelphia. Laid down on May 21, 1919, it was launched on October 18, 1919. It has the distinction of being the flush-deck destroyer which remained continuously in commission longest. Commissioned on April 20, 1920, it remained continuously in service until July 28, 1945.

Edwards spent a stretch in the Mediterranean and Black Sea from May 1920 to May 1921, three years from 1925 to 1927 conducting training cruises out of Norfolk, and two years in 1928–29 on the West Coast. *Edwards* was part of the Asiatic Fleet from 1921 to 1925 and from August 1929 until March 1942, when the Asiatic Fleet was dissolved.

Edwards carried relief supplies to Japan after the 1923 earthquake, protected foreigners during the Chinese Civil War in 1924, and after 1937 guarded American interests during the Sino-Japanese War. After Pearl Harbor, *Edwards* was part of the ABDA Command in the Java Sea. It fought at the battle of Balikpapan on February 20, 1942, and the battle of Java Sea on February 27 the same year. One of four flush-deck destroyers to escape the Java Sea on March 1, 1942, *Edwards* spent the rest of the war escorting Atlantic convoys.

This plate shows *John D. Edwards* as it would have appeared in the 1920s.

Displacement:	1,215 tons (normal), 1,308 tons (full load)
Dimensions:	314ft 4.5in. x 30ft 11.5in. x 9ft 4in.
Propulsion:	2 geared steam turbines (2 shafts), 4 × 300psi boilers, 27,600shp (designed)
Speed:	35 knots
Fuel:	Oil
Crew:	8 officers, 8 petty officers, 106 sailors
Armament (1925):	4 × 4in./50-caliber guns, 1 × 3in./23-caliber antiaircraft gun, 12 × 21in. torpedo tubes (4 × 3), 2 depth charge racks

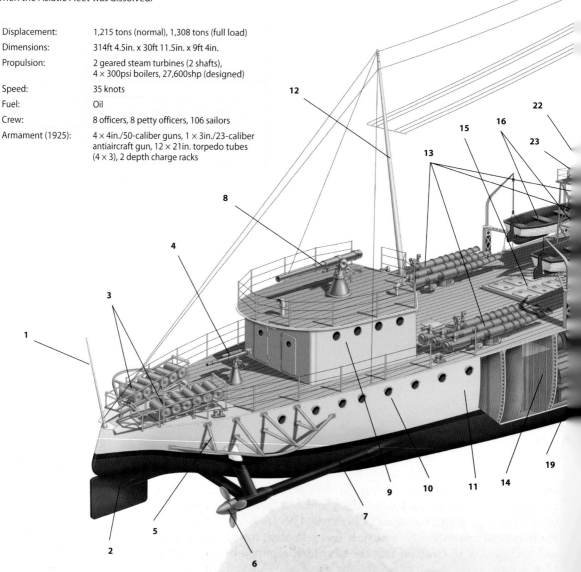

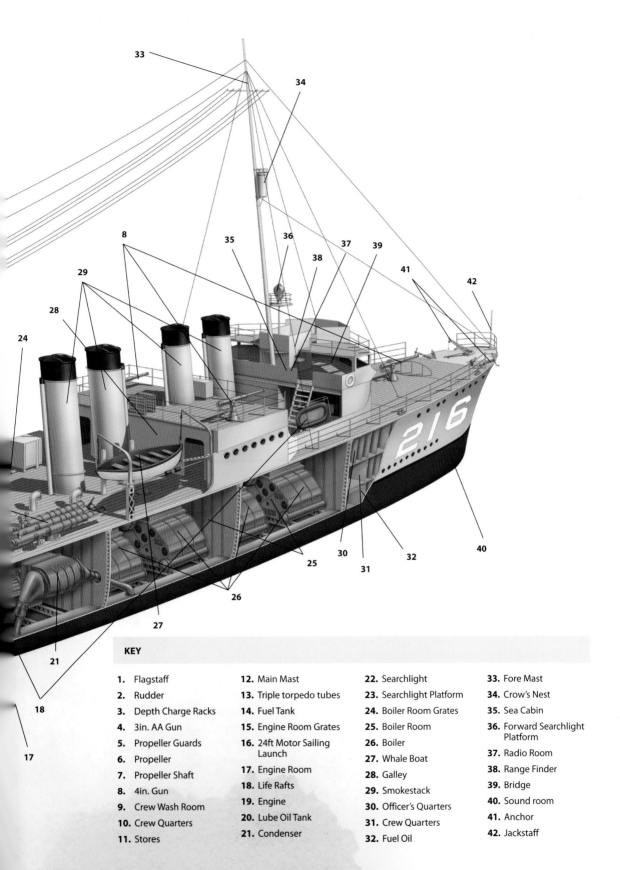

KEY

1. Flagstaff
2. Rudder
3. Depth Charge Racks
4. 3in. AA Gun
5. Propeller Guards
6. Propeller
7. Propeller Shaft
8. 4in. Gun
9. Crew Wash Room
10. Crew Quarters
11. Stores
12. Main Mast
13. Triple torpedo tubes
14. Fuel Tank
15. Engine Room Grates
16. 24ft Motor Sailing Launch
17. Engine Room
18. Life Rafts
19. Engine
20. Lube Oil Tank
21. Condenser
22. Searchlight
23. Searchlight Platform
24. Boiler Room Grates
25. Boiler Room
26. Boiler
27. Whale Boat
28. Galley
29. Smokestack
30. Officer's Quarters
31. Crew Quarters
32. Fuel Oil
33. Fore Mast
34. Crow's Nest
35. Sea Cabin
36. Forward Searchlight Platform
37. Radio Room
38. Range Finder
39. Bridge
40. Sound room
41. Anchor
42. Jackstaff

With a "return to normalcy" following World War I, most newly built flush-deck destroyers were unneeded. By 1924, most were laid up. This picture shows 77 decommissioned flush-deck destroyers and other ships awaiting future need at the 32nd Street Naval Base at San Diego, California, in 1924. (NARA)

The worst loss occurred in 1923. Fourteen destroyers from Destroyer Squadron 11 were making a high-speed run from San Francisco to San Diego on September 8, 1923. Thick fog obscured visibility. The ships steamed at 20 knots, depending on dead reckoning for navigation. When the flagship USS *Delphy* turned into what was thought to be the Santa Barbara Channel, the ship was several miles east of its navigated position. The destroyers steamed into rocks off Honda Point instead.

Five minutes later *Delphy* struck rocks, followed by USS *S. P. Lee*, *Young*, *Woodbury*, *Nicholas*, and *Fuller*. All were wrecked; *Young* capsized, *Delphy* and *Lee* broke up. *Chauncy*, attempting to rescue *Young*'s crew, ran aground and was wrecked. *Farragut* and *Somers* touched bottom, but, warned by *Delphy*'s siren, had slowed down, and worked themselves free. Five other destroyers were able to stop before grounding. They, along with local fishing

Six Clemson-class destroyers aground at Honda Point. The worst peacetime loss of ships by the US Navy, it was the biggest single-day loss of naval warships until Pearl Harbor on December 7, 1941. (USNHHC)

boats, rescued the shipwreck survivors. In all, seven Clemson-class destroyers were lost and 23 sailors died. It was the worst peacetime loss in United States Navy history.

Starting in 1929, another set of flush-deck destroyers was struck from Navy rolls due to construction flaws and diplomacy. The Yarrow boilers installed in the destroyers built in Bethlehem Steel shipyards proved to have a short lifespan. Replacing them was too expensive, especially as the country entered the Depression and naval limitations treaties constrained the numbers of destroyers.

Sixty destroyers with Yarrow boilers and ten years' active service were ordered to be scrapped. All destroyers ordered to be scrapped were in commission, and were replaced by ships in reserve. Most discarded ships went straight to the breakers. Two, USS *Preston* and *Bruce*, were used for hull-strength research. Placed in drydock, they were deliberately buckled to learn more about hogging and sagging. Lessons from these tests were applied to the next generation of destroyers.

Four others – USS *Putnam*, *Worden*, *Dale*, and *Osborne* – were purchased by the Standard Fruit Company. Re-engined with diesels, they were converted to banana boats. Another Clemson-class ship, *Moody*, was sold to MGM. MGM altered it to look like an Imperial German Navy destroyer, and sank the ship filming the 1933 war movie *Hell Below*.

Another 35 flush-deckers were ordered to be disposed of in 1935 under the terms of the London Naval Limitations Treaty. Thirty-two were broken up. Three, USS *Taylor, Walker*, and *Turner*, were still awaiting disposal when the order was reversed. They survived to serve in World War II, but not as destroyers. Finally, USS *Smith Thompson* was sunk in 1936 after being rammed by *Whipple*. Repairing her was viewed as uneconomical.

Service for surviving flush-deckers in the 1930s was more routine and generally less exciting than in the previous decade. New construction replaced the old destroyers in the battle fleets and Depression-era austerity limited Navy operations. Only the flush-deckers of the Asiatic Fleet and later Squadron 40T (created in 1936 to protect US interests during the

By the mid-1930s, the main use for the flush-deck destroyers as fleet destroyers was with the Asiatic Fleet in the Far East. Here six flush-deck destroyers of the Asiatic Fleet are tied up to destroyer tender *Black Hawk* in the Chinese port of Chefoo in 1936. These are (left to right): *John D. Ford* (DD-228), *Paul Jones* (DD-230), *Smith Thompson* (DD-212), *John D. Edwards* (DD-216), *Barker* (DD-213), and *Whipple* (DD-217). (USNHHC)

Spanish Civil War) saw action. But the Spanish Civil War and the Second Sino-Japanese War, which started in 1937, marked the opening of a new global conflict.

World War II: 1939–45

On September 1, 1939, Germany invaded Poland, starting a war which grew to a world-wide conflagration. It ended six years later, on September 2, 1945. When the flush-deck destroyers were built during World War I, they were outdated; by 1939 they approached obsolescence. Yet they were still valuable. Despite their age, many had relatively little sea service during the years they were preserved against future need. They were fast ships with sturdy hulls. Over six years, these ships saw extensive service in virtually every role imaginable: convoy escorts, seaplane tenders, mine warfare ships, fast transports, training ships, research vessels, and, briefly, in their designed function as torpedo attack platforms.

Even before World War II, the Navy took steps to bring mothballed flush-deckers into service. Early in 1939 it began a survey of the decommissioned destroyers' condition. This was followed by a program to fix material deficiencies. This program harvested its first fruits with President Franklin D. Roosevelt's "destroyers for bases" agreement in 1940. Fifty flush-deck destroyers drawn from the pool of reconditioned vessels were lent to Britain in exchange for US bases on Britain's American possessions.

In Royal Navy service these ships became the "Town" class. The ships were all named after towns in the United States and Britain that shared a common name. The lent ships let Britain fill a critical shortage of destroyers early in World War II. The British often rearmed these ships to improve their antiaircraft and antisubmarine capabilities, removing torpedo tubes, adding 20mm antiaircraft guns, extra Y-gun launchers and later Hedgehog antisubmarine mortars. Hedgehogs sometimes replaced the forward main gun. Another modification involved removing the after boiler and replacing it with a fuel-oil tank to create a long-range escort.

USS *BABBITT* (DD-128), 1944

In December 1940, the Navy's General Board ordered a modernization of the surviving flush-deck destroyers to improve their antiaircraft and antisubmarine capabilities. The aft torpedo tubes and all 4in./50-caliber and 3in./23-caliber guns were removed, replaced by six 3in./50-caliber dual-purpose guns. The aft depth-charge racks were lengthened and a Y-gun depth-charge thrower was added. Twenty-seven ships, including *Babbitt*, were completed by December 7, 1941, when the war ended this program.

Additional work was done in 1942 and 1943. On many, the after boiler and smokestack were removed and replaced with a fuel-oil tank, increasing the range by 30 percent. More light antiaircraft guns were added, with .50-caliber machine guns replaced by 20mm Oerlikons. Antisubmarine capability was added, with new K-gun depth charge launchers and Hedgehog mortars.

Babbitt showed the ultimate result of this evolution by 1944, as seen here. Its distinctive "four-pipe" silhouette now has three stacks. Its battery of six 3in./50-cal. guns has been augmented by four single 20mm guns. The Y-gun launcher aft of the after deckhouse has been replaced by two K-gun launchers, and two more K-gun launchers are installed by the waist 3in./50-cal. guns. A Hedgehog mortar sits aft of the forward 3in./50-cal. gun. Air and ground search radar antenna are on the foremast.

Babbitt wears Camouflage Measure 2, a dark gray lower hull and medium gray upper hull. The dividing line runs diagonally from mid-hull in the bow to the deck at the stern, in the hope of making the ship appear to be moving faster than it actually is.

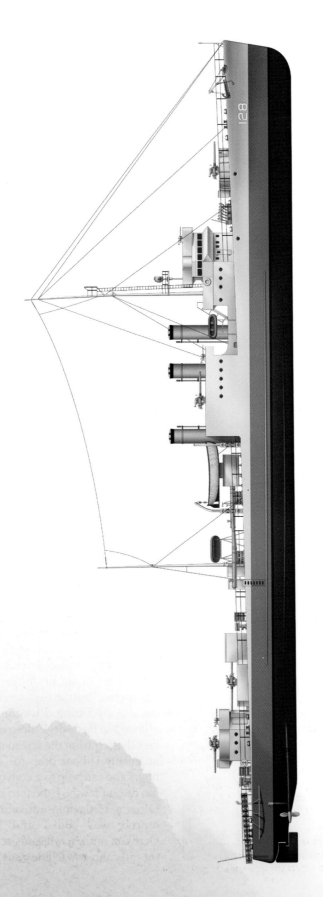
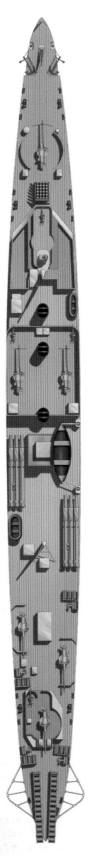

The Clemson-class destroyer *McCook* (DD-252) was one of 50 flush-deck destroyers traded to Great Britain in 1940. It is shown here at Reykjavik, Iceland, during 1941 as HMCS *St Croix*, while serving in the Royal Canadian Navy. (USNHHC)

USS *Ward* (DD-139) fired the US Navy's first shots of World War II using this 4in. gun to sink a Japanese mini-submarine attempting to enter Pearl Harbor. This photograph has the gun's crew posing by the gun. The gun is preserved today as a war monument in Minneapolis, Minnesota, where most of *Ward*'s crew came from. (USNHHC)

Town-class ships served mainly in the North Atlantic and Arctic as convoy escorts. A few wandered further afield, serving in the Middle East and Indian Ocean. Some were lent to other Allied navies, serving under Canadian, Norwegian, Dutch, and Soviet colors.

Many were decommissioned in late 1944 and 1945, replaced by new constructions. While active they provided valuable service. One, HMS *Niagara*, captured U-570. Five Town-class ships were sunk in combat. A sixth, HMS *Campbeltown*, was expended during the St Nazaire Raid, used to ram the Normandie Lock.

During its 1940 and 1941 build-up, the US Navy began commissioning laid-up flush-deck destroyers. These destroyers were little changed from their World War I configuration. Sonar had been added between the wars, and some had more Y-guns added. Major modifications began in December 1940. The aft pair of torpedo tubes and the main battery were removed, replaced with 6 3in./50-caliber dual-purpose guns. The 3in./23-caliber gun was replaced with a Y-gun. Thirty-seven were scheduled for conversion, but only 27 were completed before the war started and the program ended.

Later, to improve range, one boiler was removed on many flush-deckers and replaced with a fuel tank. They could no longer reach 35 knots, but many were well capable of hitting 30 knots. This allowed a flush-deck destroyer to detach itself from the screen to keep an enemy U-boat deep for several hours and catch up to a convoy now too distant for the U-boat to pursue. Often a Hedgehog antisubmarine mortar was added and 20mm Oerlikon antiaircraft guns replaced the .50-caliber machine guns.

Initially most flush-deckers were used as destroyers. Thirteen were assigned to the Asiatic Fleet, a number that had held steady since the 1920s. Others were assigned to escort groups in the Atlantic, part of the Neutrality Patrol organized by President Roosevelt in 1941. Each escort group had one or two flush-deckers. A few were assigned to naval bases in the Pacific and Caribbean, providing antisubmarine security around ports such as Panama and Pearl Harbor.

Flush-deck destroyers engaged in combat on several occasions before US entry into World War II, including the *Greer* Incident in September 1940 when a U-boat fired on the USS *Greer* in the North Atlantic in the mistaken belief it had launched a depth-charge attack on it, and the sinking of the *Reuben James* in October 1941 with the loss of over 100 crew. A flush-deck destroyer also fired the first shot of the Pacific War. On December 7, 1941, while guarding the entrance to the Pearl Harbor naval base off Oahu, USS *Ward* spotted the conning tower of an unknown submarine in the forbidden zone. *Ward* opened fire, striking and sinking a Japanese midget submarine sneaking into Pearl Harbor in advance of the Japanese air raid that day.

The United States declared war on Japan the next day. Germany declared war on the United States three days later, on December 11, and the war became global. Flush-deck destroyers were thrown into the fight wherever it was fought.

In the Pacific, the initial fighting fell on the flush-deck destroyers of the Asiatic Fleet. More modern destroyers filled fleet escort roles in the rest of the Pacific. The obsolescent flush-deckers had been retained in the Far East instead of stationing newer, more valuable ships in this exposed position. Withdrawn from Chinese waters in late 1941, these flush-deckers were in the Philippines when the war started. Over the next three months they waged an unequal battle against the Japanese Navy.

Japanese air power and landings on Luzon made Manila untenable. The Asiatic Fleet was withdrawn to the Dutch East Indies. There it became part of the ABDA (American, British, Dutch, Australian) command. Between January and March 1941, these 13 destroyers were thrown against the advancing Japanese.

Eight-inch shells from Japanese cruisers sink USS *Pope*. *Pope* survived the battle of the Java Sea to be trapped by the Japanese escorting the damaged British cruiser *Exeter* out of the Java Sea. (USNHHC)

Four participated in a night torpedo attack against an anchored invasion fleet at Balikpapan on Borneo. Flush-deck destroyers fought with the ABDA Fleet at the battle of Java Sea, launching torpedoes at Japanese ships. Four, USS *Edsall*, *Peary*, *Pillsbury*, and *Pope*, were sunk. One, USS *Stewart*, was scuttled in drydock, but salvaged by the Japanese. By March, the rest were withdrawn. With the exception of a handful serving as convoy escorts between Alaska and the West Coast of America, the Java Sea campaign was the last stand of the flush-deckers as destroyers in the Pacific. They served in auxiliary roles thereafter, refitted as fast transports, minesweepers, or seaplane tenders.

The reason they were not used as destroyers in the Pacific was less due to their age than their deficient antiaircraft capabilities and short range. The main function of the fleet destroyer had become serving as the antiaircraft screen for battle groups. Even after augmenting the antiaircraft batteries, flush-deck destroyers were incapable of keeping up with the fast carrier groups in the Pacific. They soldiered on as destroyers in the Atlantic, particularly on the North Atlantic run, where the shorter distances and slower convoy speeds put less stress on flush-deck range limitations.

During Operation *Torch* in November 1942, three flush-deckers – USS *Cole*, *Bernadou*, and *Dallas* - were stripped of all excess gear and sent to land troops in the heavily defended French African port of Safi prior to the main invasion. *Cole* and *Bernadou* landed troops who seized port facilities before they could be destroyed. *Dallas* steamed 8 miles up the Sebou River and landed Rangers, who captured a French airfield. The ships were picked specifically because they were viewed as expendable. All three survived the mission and the war, returning to convoy duties, eventually being scrapped in 1945.

Flush-deck destroyers provided convoy protection during the dark days of 1942 and 1943, when it was most needed. In addition to providing convoy escorts, flush-deck destroyers were part of hunter-killer groups in the Atlantic working with escort carriers.

Flush-deck destroyers sank or participated in the sinking of six U-boats during the Battle of the Atlantic, including one sunk in May 1945 off Block Island, Rhode Island, by USS *Semmes*, then serving as the sonar school ship at New London, Connecticut. In addition to *Ruben James*, U-boats sank three flush-deckers: USS *Jacob Jones*, *Leary*, and *Borie*. The last sank after ramming and sinking U-405. USS *Truxton* was wrecked off Newfoundland and *Sturtevant* sank after striking a "friendly" mine off Key West.

After the war

By the war's end only a handful of flush-deckers were still used as destroyers. Many had been converted to auxiliaries, seeing extensive service in the Pacific. Their story is related later. As new construction poured out of American shipyards,

In 1941, 27 flush-deck destroyers, including *Roper* (DD-147), were converted to escort destroyers. This shows the changes involved, including the removal of the aft torpedo tubes, replaced by depth-charge launchers and 3in./50-cal. antiaircraft guns, and replacement of the 4in. main guns with 3in./50-cal. guns. *Roper* retains its after funnel and boiler in this photo. (USNHHC)

many flush-deckers were re-rated as gunboats or simply retired. It was easier to convert new construction to the auxiliary roles filled by the flush-deck ships than keep the older ships in commission. By September 2, 1945, 76 flush-deckers were still in commission in the United States Navy, with only four still rated as destroyers.

The surviving ships were retired as soon as they reached an American shipyard – or even in a few cases in the place where they were stationed. Most were gone and heading to the scrapyard by the end of 1945; the rest were decommissioned in 1946. The last to go was USS *Bulmer*, a survivor of the Java Sea campaign, which was decommissioned on August 16, 1946. By 1947, all had been broken up for scrap or sunk as targets.

The latter included USS *Stewart*, presumed destroyed at Surabaya on Java in 1942. The Japanese salvaged it, re-commissioning it Patrol Boat No. 102 in September 1943. The ex-*Stewart* survived the war, and was reclaimed following Japan's surrender. Since a new *Stewart* was by then in the United States Navy, the prize was designated RAMP-224, towed back to California, and sunk as a target on May 24, 1946.

Survivors of the 50 Town-class destroyers lent to Great Britain lasted a little longer. The British phased out theirs almost as fast as the US Navy, but took longer to break them up. The final ones lasted until 1949 and were broken up in Great Britain. Late in the war, Britain lent nine Town-class destroyers to the Soviets. The Soviets hung on to them after the war ended, but they returned most to Britain in 1949; these were scrapped as they arrived. One other was returned in 1951, and the final two, *Zhivuchiy*

While serving in the Aleutians, USS *Hulbert* (then AVP-6) was forced ashore by a storm. The ship was pulled off and repaired, closing the war as an airplane guard. (USNHHC)

USS *Stewart* was salvaged by the Japanese at Surabaya and converted to a patrol boat. Recovered by the United States Navy at the end of World War II, the ship was returned to the United States and expended as a target ship in April 1946. (USNHHC)

(ex-USS *Fairfax*, ex-HMS *Richmond*) and *Druzhny* (ex-USS *Yarnall*, ex-HMS *Lincoln*), returned in 1952.

There was one last flush-decker remaining – *Teapa*, one of the four flush-deckers converted to fruit boats in the 1930s. One had been wrecked in 1933. The three survivors were used as fast cargo ships during the war, and two were lost. USS *Teapa*, formerly *Putnam*, survived the war and returned to carrying bananas between 1947 and 1950. In 1950 she was laid up, being tied up until 1955, when she was sold for scrap.

VARIANTS

The numbers in which flush-deck destroyers were constructed meant the United States Navy always had more destroyers than could be used with the fleet, even right after the ships were built. As they aged and naval warfare changed, the flush-deck destroyers became less capable of serving as fleet destroyers. Yet the Navy had need for fast auxiliary ships, never more so than immediately after Pearl Harbor. Building auxiliaries required shipyard space desperately needed for new warships.

The flush-deck destroyers offered a solution to this problem. They were fast, sturdy vessels, but surplus to Navy needs for fleet destroyers. Converting an existing hull with a working propulsion system to a new function took significantly less time than building a new ship. The Navy took full advantage of the opportunity offered by the flush-deck destroyers, and over 90 were converted to auxiliary warships.

There were three major roles for which flush-deck destroyers were converted to serve: as mine warfare ships, as seaplane tenders and aviation

E

THE *GREER* INCIDENT

On September 4, 1941, USS *Greer*, a Wickes-class destroyer, was carrying mail and passengers to Iceland. At the time, *Greer* was part of the Neutrality Patrol, enforcing a neutrality zone in the Western Atlantic unilaterally declared by President Franklin D. Roosevelt. The United States was a non-belligerent; its ships could not attack German vessels, except in self-defense – if fired upon first.

Informed of a German U-boat in the area, *Greer*'s captain began seeking it. *Greer* found the U-boat, U-652, and began tracking it, broadcasting the submarine's location. When a British aircraft dropped four depth charges on the U-boat, the submarine's commander assumed *Greer* had attacked it, and fired a torpedo in response.

Spotting the torpedo's wake, *Greer* maneuvered to avoid the torpedo, which missed astern. *Greer* then maneuvered to the assumed position of the U-boat and dropped eight depth charges. Two minutes later, U-652 fired a second torpedo at *Greer*. This, too, was avoided, missing off the port beam. The *Greer*'s commander, J.J. Mahoney, then began a systematic search for the submerged U-boat, which went deep. After two hours of tracking and unsuccessfully attacking the U-boat a second time, dropping 11 more depth charges, Mahoney gave up the search and resumed course to Iceland.

The exchange became known as the *Greer* Incident. The United States accused Germany of an unprovoked attack on its ship. Germany responded that their submarine retaliated after being attacked by the US ship. Roosevelt declared the German action "an act of piracy" and authorized US warships to "shoot on sight" if encountering German warships in the neutrality zone. It was the first of three armed encounters between US and German warships prior to US entry into World War II.

This plate show the opening of the battle, as the track of the first torpedo passes astern of the accelerating and maneuvering destroyer.

vessels, and as fast troop transports. In all, 22 flush-deck destroyers were converted to minelayers, 18 to minesweepers, 14 to seaplane tenders, and 32 to fast attack transports.

A few were converted to other functions. Three flush-deckers – USS *Stoddert*, *Lamberton*, and *Boggs* – who had been removed from Navy rolls due to the London Treaty, were demilitarized, stripped of their armament and fitted with funnel shields and radio-control equipment. They served as mobile targets for aircraft, steaming and maneuvering by remote control. *Stoddert* and *Lamberton* were scrapped in the 1930s. *Boggs*, along with *Kilty*, selected for the program

USS *Stoddert* was demilitarized as a result of the 1930 London Treaty and transformed into a radio-controlled target ship, as shown here. The funnel covers were intended to prevent practice bombs from damaging the boilers. (USNHHC)

but never converted, survived until World War II, returning to commission as warships.

Six flush-deckers were converted to Coast Guard cutters in the 1930s. Their torpedo tubes and depth charges were removed, and they chased down rum runners until Prohibition ended. All reverted to the Navy by 1937. *Semmes* was selected as the Navy's underwater sound experimental ship in 1934. It served in that role or as a sonar school ship until it was decommissioned in 1946. *Turner*, converted to a self-propelled water barge due to the London Treaty, later became an experimental ship. Renamed *Moosehead*, it trained radar operators and pioneered Combat Information Center development. *Walker*, also demilitarized, was converted to a damage-

BATTLE OF BALIKPAPAN

The flush-deck destroyer was designed to launch a surface torpedo attack against enemy ships, built around its torpedo tubes. Yet the battle of Balikpapan was the only action where flush-deck destroyers served as torpedo platforms.

After the Japanese invaded Borneo at Balikpapan, the available destroyers of the Asiatic Fleet – USS *Paul Jones*, *Parrott*, *Pope*, and *John D. Ford* – were sent to attack the invasion fleet. They arrived at Balikpapan Harbor shortly after 2:30 am on February 24, 1942. Anchored in the harbor were 12 transports. Shortly before the Americans arrived, the Japanese Fleet's destroyer escort was sent out of the harbor seeking an already departed Dutch submarine. Three patrol craft remained to guard the transports.

The Japanese were silhouetted against the glow of burning refineries to the north, whereas the US ships were invisible in the moonless dark. The destroyers steamed in line ahead at 27 knots. Maneuvering through the Japanese, the destroyers fired torpedoes at the Japanese ships they passed. They fired torpedoes individually or in pairs. It was a confused melee, with the Japanese not realizing they were being attacked until their ships began exploding.

First to go was the 3,500-ton *Sumanoura Maru*, which exploded. *Tatsukami Maru*, 7,064 tons, was hit next and was sunk by one torpedo. *P-37*, a patrol boat, was sunk by torpedoes fired by *Pope* and *Parrott*. *Ford*, *Jones*, and *Pope* next took out the 5,000-ton *Kuretake Maru*. Finally, the last torpedo fired struck and sank *Nana Maru*, 6,700 tons. Out of torpedoes, the destroyers split up and opened up with their guns, damaging two more transports before they finally withdrew.

Only five ships out of 17, all anchored, were hit by the 48 torpedoes fired. The transports were empty of troops, landed earlier or in landing craft. Regardless, it was a tactical victory, and the first surface action fought by the US Navy since the Spanish-American War in 1898.

Converting a flush-deck destroyer to a minelayer involved removing the torpedo tubes and replacing them with mine-laying racks. Each rack could hold up to 40 naval mines. (USNHHC)

control training ship in 1941. In the mid-Pacific being towed to Pearl Harbor when the Japanese attacked Hawaii, *Walker* was scuttled at sea.

Mine warfare

Mine warfare was the first alternate use to which flush-deckers were put. World War I had demonstrated the usefulness of fast minelaying ships. The Royal Navy built or converted destroyers and cruisers as minelayers. These ships demonstrated how offensive minefields could shut down enemy naval ports or close strategic waterways at critical times. Facing a shortage of fast minelayers after World War I, the United States Navy decided to use surplus flush-deck destroyers for that role.

In 1920, 14 Wickes-class destroyers were converted to minelayers. The torpedo tubes and mainmast were removed, and the deck space was filled with minelaying tracks. Nothing else was altered. They kept the same boilers and engines as standard destroyers. The minelayers could keep up with their destroyer sister ships. They retained one depth-charge rack placed between the mine racks, allowing them to fulfill antisubmarine duties in the minelayer configuration. Each minelayer could carry 80 mines.

While designated with DM (for destroyer, minelayer) and numbered DM-1 through to 14, most initially kept their destroyer hull numbers. Presumably this was because they could quickly become destroyers by removing the mine tracks and replacing the main mast and torpedo tubes.

Six of these 14 original minelayers had Yarrow boilers, and were among the 60 flush-deckers scrapped in 1930. Four replacements were commissioned, converted from laid-up flush-deck destroyers. The remaining eight original minelayers were scrapped in 1936 and 1937, and four more replacements added from the mothballed fleet.

The United States Navy entered World War II with eight flush-deck minelayers. All were stationed at Pearl Harbor on December 7. They spent the rest of the war in the Pacific. Five were sent to the Solomons and three to the Aleutians in 1942 and 1943, and sowed mines in both theaters. Mines they laid off Guadalcanal and in the Blackett Strait during 1943 sank two Japanese destroyers and crippled two others. These two were sunk later by Allied aircraft. Minefields laid in the Aleutians were less successful, sinking no Japanese ships.

Their activities were not limited to minelaying. They performed a variety of other duties, including leading landing craft to beaches, and on occasion doubling up as minesweepers. USS *Gamble* depth-charged I-123 on August 29, 1942. Another minelayer, USS *Tracy*, became the first Allied ship to enter Nagasaki Harbor in Japan.

Two were lost. USS *Preble* hit a drifting mine off Palau in October 1944, and *Gamble* was hit by a 250lb bomb in an air attack off Iwo Jima. Neither sank, but both were so badly damaged that they were not worth repairing.

In 1940, the Navy realized any war would require amphibious invasions. This prompted conversion of flush-deck destroyers to minesweepers. Enemy minefields off invasion beaches required fast minesweepers, as slow ones could be deterred by shore batteries. *Manley* had been experimentally converted in 1935, but the sweeping gear was removed shortly afterwards. In 1940, eight destroyers were converted.

The initial minelayer conversions retained all four boilers and funnels. By World War II, some minelayers had the after funnel and boiler removed, replaced by a fuel tank for additional range. (AC)

This was more involved than the minelayer conversions, since the torpedo tubes were removed. To make room for sweeping davits, a false stern was added over the knife-edge cruiser stern of the production classes. (*Manley*'s cutaway stern, characteristic of the Caldwell-class, was one reason the Navy used *Manley* for the conversion test in 1935.)

The depth-charge racks were retained but were moved, now angled over the propeller guards. A massive cable winch was placed behind the aft deckhouse and paravanes added. The aft boiler and funnel were removed and replaced with a fuel tank. This change was made to add range rather than for minesweeping purposes. The first set of conversions replaced the low-angle 4in./50-caliber main battery with 3in./50-caliber dual-purpose guns and 20mm antiaircraft guns were added.

The Navy was so pleased with the result that ten more flush-deckers were converted in 1941 for a total of 18 DMS (Destroyer-Mine Sweeper) vessels. This total excludes the famous but fictional USS *Caine*, the setting for Herman Wouk's novel *The Caine Mutiny*. The novel was based on the author's wartime experiences aboard two actual flush-decker minesweepers, USS *Zane* and *Southard*.

Some 1941 conversions retained their 4in./50-caliber guns, although light antiaircraft guns were added to improve air defense. Radar was added as it became available. The sweep gear initially installed only worked on moored mines, with paravanes used to stream a cable that snagged moored mines. Equipment was added with the capability to sweep for magnetic and acoustic mines. Since this gear drank electricity, the three 25Kw generators normally carried by flush-deck vessels were replaced with two 60Kw units.

When the United States entered World War II, eight flush-deck DMSs were in commission, four in the Atlantic and four in the Pacific. The four Atlantic vessels did some minesweeping during Operation *Torch*, clearing beaches off Casablanca and Fedhala. Most of their duties involved convoy escort and antisubmarine warfare. They were transferred to the Pacific in December 1943 as the pace of amphibious operations picked up.

The four DMSs in the Pacific spent 1942 and 1943 mostly in the Southwest Pacific supporting the Solomons campaign and in the Aleutians. Two, USS *Long* and *Southard*, each sank a Japanese submarine during 1942. In addition to minesweeping, the ships were used for everything that

The conversion of flush-deck destroyers to fast minesweepers was an experiment by the United States Navy. It proved so successful the Navy began converting newer destroyers and destroyer escorts, replacing most of the flush-deck conversions. This picture shows USS *Hogan*. (AC)

needed doing: fire support, towing, surveying, sea rescue, and occasionally to transport marine raiding parties.

In 1944 and 1945, they participated in pre-invasion minesweeping and beach clearing operations. Often they worked with APDs (flush-deckers converted to troop carriers) which carried Underwater Demolition Teams to assist in clearing obstacles. Five DMSs were present at Palau and ten at Lingayen Gulf, where they swept the beaches in advance of the landing forces.

Five flush-deck DMSs were lost during World War II and two immediately after it ended. USS *Wasmuth* sank after its depth charges were swept off the ship during a storm in the Aleutians and blew up under her stern. Most of the crew was saved, but the ship sank on December 27, 1942. USS *Perry* struck a mine and sank off Palau. USS *Hovey*, *Long*, and *Palmer* were sunk at Lingayen Gulf by Japanese aircraft. USS *Dorsey* and *Southard* survived the war, only to be caught in a typhoon off Okinawa in October 1945. Both were driven aground on October 9, and the ships stricken and scrapped.

Only three remained in service as minesweepers on V-J Day, including *Dorsey* and *Southard*. The other ten had been replaced by later construction. The Navy converted 24 Benson- and Gleaves-class destroyers to DMSs in 1944 and 1945. This allowed the flush-deck conversions to be retired to easier duties – training and target towing. As with their destroyer minelayer sisters, the flush-deck destroyer minesweepers provided valuable service during World War II, filling a role less glamorous than that of a fleet destroyer, but just as important.

Conversion to a minelayer involved adding a false stern to hold the minesweeping davits, adding a winch on the fantail, a cable-spool forward of the aft deckhouse, and angling the depth-charge racks over the propeller guards. This photograph of USS *Zane* shows these changes. (USNHHC)

Aviation service

From the time of the first transatlantic flight in 1919, when 21 flush-deck destroyers served as plane guides for NC-1, NC-3, and NC-4, the Navy used flush-deck destroyers in cooperation with naval aviation. This included experiments using flush-deckers as seaplane carriers and culminated in 14 serving as seaplane tenders during World War II.

The first use of flush-deckers as aviation ships was in late 1919.

Two flush-deckers, USS *Harding* and *Mugford*, were converted to seaplane tenders. The conversion was rudimentary. The after torpedo tubes were removed and replaced with gasoline tanks. The two ships operated out of Pensacola, Florida, as part of the Air Detachment, Atlantic Fleet. They participated in training naval aviators and also supported seaplane operations in the Caribbean. *Harding* was also present at the July 1921 tests off Hampton Roads when demobilized US Navy warships and prize ships from the Imperial German Navy were bombed by aircraft. *Harding* and *Mugford* served as seaplane tenders until the spring of 1922, when they were laid up. Both were scrapped in 1936 as a result of the London Treaty.

The next flush-decker associated with naval aviation was USS *Charles Ausburn*. In 1923, a cradle was added forward, between the bow 4in. gun and the bridge, capable of carrying the TS-1 scout aircraft used on the aircraft carrier *Langley*. A floatplane version was placed on *Charles Ausburn*. Also added were fuel tanks and cranes allowing the TS-1 to be hoisted between the cradle and the water.

Over the next several months the ship and aircraft operated with the Scouting Fleet in the Atlantic, testing the feasibility of operating aircraft off destroyers. The experiment was considered successful, although a major recommendation was that aircraft on destroyers be located on the quarterdeck rather than the forecastle. The aircraft and equipment were removed by April 1924. The experiment was not repeated until 1940, and for 16 years naval aviation managed without using destroyers.

Interest resumed after World War II started but before the US entered the conflict. When the Clemson-class USS *Noa* was recommissioned in April 1940, the after torpedo tubes were removed and an aircraft platform fitted just forward of the aft deckhouse. The mainmast was replaced with a boom to lift the seaplane into and out of the water. A Curtiss Seagull seaplane was carried and trial operations conducted in May 1940. The results were promising, so much so that six Fletcher-class destroyers were fitted with a catapult and a Kingfisher floatplane. Results were ultimately unsatisfactory, however, and the program was abandoned. By that time, *Noa* had removed its seaplane and been converted to a fast attack transport.

While launching aircraft off destroyers never worked, operating aircraft from destroyers was more successful. In 1940, the Navy increased its patrol bomber squadrons significantly. Each squadron had 12 aircraft, typically PBY Catalina amphibians. They could operate independently of shore facilities using a seaplane tender for maintenance, fuel, and supplies. A standard tender supported two squadrons, but the Navy had so many new patrol areas they were building light seaplane tenders to support single-squadron patrol areas.

One of the earliest experiments with deploying aircraft on destroyers was conducted in 1923, when a TR-1 floatplane was mounted on the *Charles Ausburn*. The aircraft can be seen forward of the bridge, aft of the forward 4in. gun. (USNHHC)

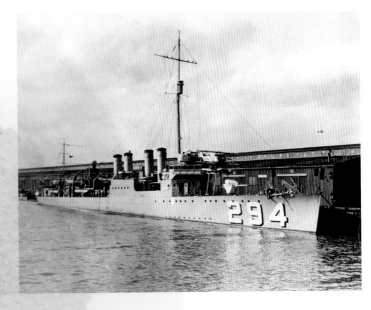

The experiment was repeated in April 1940, when a Seagull floatplane was mounted on the after deck of USS *Noa* (DD-343). As a result, its crew adopted an image of cartoon-character Popeye flying a winged spinach can as the ship's insignia. (USNHHC)

New construction of light seaplane tenders lagged the need for tenders. The Navy converted flush-deck destroyers to fill this gap. The Navy experimentally converted the Clemson-class USS *Childs* and *Williamson* in 1938. The torpedo tubes, the two waist 4in. guns and the 3in./32-caliber antiaircraft gun were removed. The depth-charge racks were retained and Y-gun throwers added to those lacking them, retaining their antisubmarine capabilities.

The forward two boilers and smokestacks were removed. The forward deckhouse was expanded, adding officers' cabins, crew quarters, and office space for the aviation personnel. The boiler space was converted to fuel storage. Tanks carrying 30,000 gallons of aviation gasoline were installed. A crane was fitted amidships, and an aircraft homing beacon attached to the mast. Radar was added during the war, as it became available.

These ships could not hoist a Catalina aboard, so maintenance was done in the water. Two boats were added for servicing aircraft. The first two were ready by 1939 and used in that year's fleet problem. The Navy was pleased with their performance, ordering seven mothballed and five commissioned flush-deckers converted to light seaplane tenders. Initially these carried an AVP hull number, but this was changed to AVD in 1940 to differentiate them from the minesweeper conversions and purpose-built light seaplane tenders.

Since the main function of the Catalina squadrons supported by these seaplane tenders was reconnaissance, and good reconnaissance demanded as wide a coverage net as possible, these 14 ships usually operated individually, in scattered locations. When World War II started, six AVD were in the Atlantic, six were in the Pacific, and two were assigned to the Asiatic Fleet.

The six in the Atlantic were scattered in duty locations ranging from Recife in Brazil to Reykjavik, Iceland. USS *Clemson*, *Osmond Ingram*, and *Greene* spent the first year of the war in the Caribbean and South Atlantic. *George F. Badger*, *Goldsborough*, and *Belknap* were assigned to Argentia and Reykjavik. Their Catalinas hunted U-boats. In 1943, when the need for antisubmarine vessels became critical, five seaplane tenders were attached to

Fourteen flush-deck destroyers were converted to light seaplane tenders in 1939 and 1940. They had an enlarged bridge structure for the aviation crew. They were also distinguished by the missing forward stacks and the boats for servicing floatplanes. (USNHHC)

hunter-killer groups built around the escort carriers USS *Bogue* and *Core*. They remained in this role through early 1944, when they were reassigned to the Pacific.

Three of the Pacific fleet AVDs were in Hawaii on December 7, 1941. Three others were on the Pacific Coast at San Diego in California, Puget Sound, and Yakutat Bay in Alaska. The two Asiatic Fleet vessels were in the Philippines.

The two in the Philippines, USS *Childs* and *William B. Preston*, were chased out by the Japanese advance, escaping to Australia. They served there until 1944. USS *Hulbert* and *Williamson* operated in Alaska and the Aleutians. Two others served in the Solomons campaign. One, USS *Ballard*, temporarily abandoned its aviation role to serve as a troop transport, evacuating two Marine raider companies trapped by Japanese forces.

As purpose-built light seaplane tenders became available, the need for the AVDs declined. Even with two boilers gone, they were fast ships. Most were converted to fast attack transports, a type which proved useful, and for which demand was growing. By the war's end, only four were still AVDs: USS *Childs*, *William B. Preston*, *Ballard*, and *Gillis*. These were serving as plane guards for escort carriers training air groups at San Diego.

While serving as seaplane tenders, these ships typically had quieter wars than their counterparts serving as destroyers, escort destroyers, mine warfare ships, or fast attack transports. Only one AVD was lost while serving as an AVD. On April 5, 1945, USS *Thornton* collided with two fleet oilers during refueling operations off Okinawa. Determined to be not worth repairing, *Thornton* was stripped, beached, and decommissioned.

Fast transports

As the United States Marine Corps developed its amphibious doctrine in the 1930s, the United States Navy realized that high-speed transports capable of moving quickly to unload small units either as raiders or as the advance guard of an invasion would be needed. While troop transports were available, most were taken from conventional passenger vessels or converted cargo ships. Few were fast enough, and those that were, such as Atlantic passenger liners, were too big and too valuable to risk.

Building fast transport required propulsion machinery that could otherwise power a badly needed warship. Converting warships could work if warships both fast enough and small enough could be found whose loss as a warship would not outweigh their usefulness as a transport.

The flush-deck destroyers seemed ideal conversion candidates. While fast, they were too slow to operate with fast carrier task groups. Approaching obsolescence as destroyers, with inadequate antiaircraft capabilities, they could be sacrificed without hurting fleet operational capabilities. In 1938, the Navy used USS *Manley*,

USS *Manley* was the first flush-deck destroyer converted to a fast transport. This picture captures *Manley* in September 1940, after it had been modified, but before the US entered World War II. Note the Higgins boats in the davits. (USNHHC)

USS *Little* (APD-3) in an early "Green Dragon" camouflage scheme. It was probably one applied extemporaneously by the crew in August 1942. *Little* was lost on September 5, trapped in the Slot off Guadalcanal by a Japanese surface force. (AC)

previously used as a prototype seaplane tender and then classified as a miscellaneous auxiliary, as a prototype for a destroyer-conversion high-speed transport (APD). *Manley* was given a partial conversion, allowing it to carry 120 Marines. The experiment was successful.

In 1939, *Manley* went through a more comprehensive refit. The forward fire room was converted to accommodations for troops, with the front two boilers and smokestacks removed to make room. Also removed were all the torpedo tubes, replaced by davits to hold landing craft and four 36-foot LCPL (Landing Craft, Personnel, Large) or LCVP (Landing Craft, Vehicle Personnel) Higgins boats. The two waist guns were altered: one was removed, and the second was mounted on the centerline. The ship could carry up to 200 Marines for up to 48 hours.

Even with two boilers removed, the ADPs made a good turn of speed. Water resistance increases as the cube of the speed; nearly half of a flush-decker's horsepower went to give it its final 6 knots of speed. In theory, an APD could make 29 knots, but time had taken its toll on both hull and machinery, and 26 knots was a more typical top speed for these old ships.

In May 1940, five more APD conversions were ordered, and by December 7, 1941, six were in commission: USS *Manley*, *Colhoun*, *Gregory*, *Little*, *McKean*, and *Stringham*. Initially the six were split between the Atlantic and the Pacific. When the Allies moved to the offensive in the Solomons

G THE *MANLEY* OFF CORREGIDOR

One of the most popular uses for old flush-deck destroyers was as fast attack transports. USS *Manley*, one of the six Caldwell-class destroyers, was the first ship converted and one of the longest-lived in that role.

Manley, a combat veteran of World War I, had been outfitted as a fast troop transport (APD) in February 1939. In September 1942, *Manley* was one of six APDs sent to the Southwest Pacific to support the first Allied offensive in the Pacific, the landing at Guadalcanal. It landed troops on Guadalcanal several times during that campaign, and was one of two APDs to survive it. Later, it participated in landings at Kwajalein, Yap, Saipan, Leyte Gulf, and Luzon.

In January 1945, *Manley* was one of four APDs assigned to land troops to recapture Corregidor, captured by the Japanese in May 1942. Corregidor commanded the entrance to Manila Bay, and its control was key to reopening Manila as a harbor.

This plate shows the opening of the landing. Shortly after sunrise, *Manley* stopped at the departure point and lowered its four LCVP Higgins boats into the water. Each boat was 36ft long and could carry 36 armed troops and its four-man crew. Although Corregidor had been bombarded and bombed, hidden gun emplacements survived and took the invasion force, including *Manley*, under fire. *Manley* responded by providing fire support with its broadside of three 4in./50-cal. guns.

The ship is shown in Camouflage Measure 31, a mixture of greens and brown. This was one of a number of tropical green camouflage systems used for landing craft and fast attack transports. It was adopted in 1943, and shows the *Manley* as it would have appeared during the recapture of Corregidor on February 16, 1945. It probably sported several versions of tropical green camouflage during its service as a fast transport.

USS *Stringham* (APD-6) was the last of the prewar APD conversions, and one of two to survive the Solomons campaign. It is shown here under way in 1944, probably during the Marianas campaign, when it carried underwater demolition teams. (USNHHC)

and invaded Guadalcanal, all six were in the Southwest Pacific. They were collected into Transport Division 12, and used extensively over the next six months. They carried raiding parties, landed reinforcements where needed, and during the opening months of the Guadalcanal campaign ran critical supplies into the besieged Marine beachhead. They rescued survivors and landed guerillas throughout the Solomon chain.

To better camouflage these ships at island ports, these APDs were given a mottled green paint scheme, as were future APDs. The class gained the nickname "Green Dragons." The paint job was insufficient protection, however, and between August 1942 and November 1943 four of these six ships – *Colhoun*, *Gregory*, *Little*, and *McKean* – were sunk by Japanese warships and aircraft.

Yet even by September 1942, the class had proved its usefulness. In October 1942, the Navy ordered six more flush-deck destroyers converted. Between November 1942 and June 1944, an additional 24 flush-deck destroyers were converted to APDs, bringing the total to 36. In this total were six AVPs, converted from seaplane tenders to fast transports as the need for light seaplane tenders dropped as new purpose-built light seaplane tenders became available.

The conversion of nine more flush-deckers into two AVPs and seven destroyers was ordered but canceled before work began. Instead, new construction destroyers and destroyer escorts were converted to APDs while under construction. As newly built ships entered commission, older flush-decker APDs were retired. They reverted to destroyer status or general auxiliary (AG) status. There they soldiered on until the end of the war, towing targets, training, or serving as airplane guards.

However, the APDs saw a lot of action before that happened, in both the European theater and the Atlantic. USS *Kane* (not the model for the fictional *Caine*) was the only APD to serve in Alaskan waters. It landed 1st Special Service Force on Kiska. The island had been evacuated by the Japanese, and the unit transferred to Europe, where it gained fame as the Devil's Brigade in Italy.

Four APDs were sent to Europe, where they served in the Mediterranean, landing US Commandos and Free French troops on French Mediterranean islands and supporting the invasion of Southern France in August 1944. They also served as transports, couriers, and rescue ships. After the French invasions, these ships were sent to the Pacific in 1945.

In the Pacific, the APDs were just about everywhere. They supported virtually every landing in the Southwest Pacific, including operations at Bougainville, New Guinea, New Britain, and the Green Islands. Two, USS *Overton* and *Manley*, participated at the invasion of Kwajalein. While the troops landed on the wrong island, they discovered a cache of Japanese harbor charts, aiding future invasions.

Later on they were present in large numbers in operations from Palau to Okinawa. They played their most important role during Philippine operations, when they landed troops at critical points to seize strategic positions or cut off Japanese troops. This included landings at Leyte, the Bataan Peninsula, Corregidor, and Lingayan Gulf.

The APDs also supported Underwater Demolition Team (UDT) operations. UDTs were small parties of divers who cleared beach obstacles immediately prior to a landing. It required a fast ship to carry them near the beach, protect the frogmen with fire support, and then retrieve them. The flush-decker APDs were fast and had a battery of 4-inch guns. USS *Dickerson* pioneered these tactics in practice at Hawaii and put the training into action during the Marianas invasions, along with several other flush-decker APDs. The UDTs deployed off APDs for the rest of the war.

Besides the four original APDs lost, seven others became casualties. USS *Noa* collided with the destroyer *Fullham* and sank on September 12, 1944, while steaming to the Palau Islands with a UDT team. USS *Ward*, *Brooks*, and *Belknap* were hit by kamikaze aircraft during operations in the Philippines between December 1944 and January 1945. *Ward* sank; *Brooks* and *Belknap* were damaged beyond repair. *Dickerson* and *Barry* were struck by kamikazes during Okinawa activities in April and May 1945, and subsequently sank. Ironically, *Barry,* after being judged beyond repair, was being towed to a spot where it would be beached to serve as a kamikaze decoy when a second kamikaze struck and sank it. *Greene* grounded and was wrecked October 9, 1945, by a typhoon off Okinawa.

The Navy eventually converted 31 flush-deck destroyers to APDs. The final conversion was *Clemson*, the name ship of the Clemson-class. It is shown here straight out of the dockyard after conversion, before receiving camouflage paint. The circles indicate dockyard changes. (USNHHC)

BIBLIOGRAPHY

Alden, John D., *Flush Decks and Four Pipes*, Naval Institute Press, Annapolis, Maryland (1989)

Friedman, Norman, *U.S. Destroyers: An Illustrated History*, Naval Institute Press, Annapolis, Maryland (1989)

Morrison, Samuel Eliot, *History of United States Naval Operations in World War II* (15 Volumes), Little, Brown & Co, New York, New York (1984) (reissue)

Parks, O., and Prendergast, Maurice, *Jane's Fighting Ships 1919*, Sampson Low, Marston & Co. Ltd, London (1919)

Turner Publishing Company, *The Famed Green Dragons: The Four Stack APDs*, Turner Publishing, Paducah, Kentucky (1998)

Dictionary of American Naval Fighting Ships, online edition (URL: https://www.history.navy.mil/research/histories/ship-histories/danfs.html - Accessed March 1, 2017)

INDEX